Carols for Children

ILLUSTRATED BY SANDY NIGHTINGALE

MACMILLAN
CHILDREN'S BOOKS

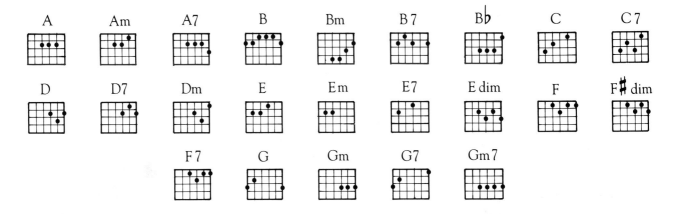

GUITAR CHORDS

First published 1988 by Macmillan Children's Books

This edition published 2002 by Macmillan Children's Books a division of Macmillan Publisher Limited
20 New Wharf Road, London N1 9RR Basingstoke and Oxford
www.panmacmillan.com

Associated companies throughout the world

ISBN 0 330 35164 8

3 5 7 9 8 6 4

A CIP catalogue record for this book is available from the British Library.

Printed in the United Kingdom by Henry Ling Limited, at the Dorset Press, Dorchester, DT1 1HD

Contents

We Wish You a Merry Christmas

1. We wish you a mer – ry Christ – mas, We wish you a mer – ry Christmas, We wish you a mer – ry Christmas, And a hap – py New Year.

CHORUS
Good ti – dings we bring To you and your kin, We wish you a mer – ry Christ – mas, And a hap – py New Year.

2. Now bring us some figgy pudding,
   Now bring us some figgy pudding,
   Now bring us some figgy pudding,
   And bring some out here.
   Chorus

3. For we all like figgy pudding,
   For we all like figgy pudding,
   For we all like figgy pudding,
   So bring some out here.
   Chorus

4. And we won't go until we've had some,
   And we won't go until we've had some,
   And we won't go until we've had some,
   So bring some out here.
   Chorus

It Came upon a Midnight Clear

1. It＿ came upon a ＿ midnight clear That glorious song of old, From＿
an－gels bend－ing near the earth To＿ touch their harps of gold: 'Peace
on the earth, good will to men, From heav'n's all－grac－ious King!' The
world in sol－emn＿ stillness lay To＿ hear＿ the ang－els sing.

2. Still through the cloven skies they come,
   With peaceful wings unfurled;
   And still their heavenly music floats
   O'er all the weary world:
   Above its sad and lowly plains
   They bend on hovering wing;
   And ever o'er its Babel-sounds
   The blessèd angels sing.

3. Yet with the woes of sin and strife
   The world has suffered long;
   Beneath the angel-strain have rolled
   Two thousand years of wrong;
   And man, at war with man, hears not
   The love-song which they bring:
   O hush the noise, ye men of strife,
   And hear the angels sing.

4. And ye, beneath life's crushing load,
   Whose forms are bending low,
   Who toil along the climbing way
   With painful steps and slow,
   Look now! for glad and golden hours
   Come swiftly on the wing;
   O rest beside the weary road,
   And hear the angels sing.

5. For lo, the days are hastening on,
   By prophet-bards foretold,
   When, with the ever-circling years,
   Comes round the age of gold;
   When peace shall over all the earth
   Its ancient splendours fling,
   And the whole world give back the song
   Which now the angels sing.

Good King Wenceslas

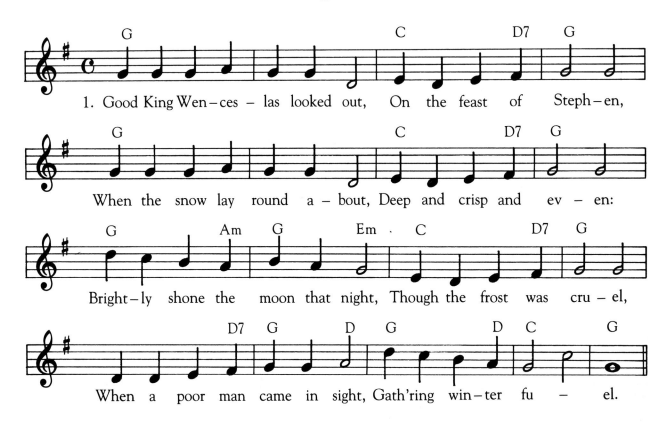

2. 'Hither page and stand by me,
   If thou knowest it, telling,
   Yonder peasant who is he?
   Where and what his dwelling?'
   'Sire, he lives a good league hence,
   Underneath the mountain,
   Right against the forest fence,
   By St Agnes fountain.'

3. 'Bring me flesh and bring me wine,
   Bring me pine logs hither:
   Thou and I will see him dine,
   When we bear them thither.'
   Page and monarch, forth they went,
   Forth they went together;
   Through the rude wind's wild lament
   And the bitter weather.

4. 'Sire, the night is darker now,
   And the wind blows stronger;
   Fails my heart, I know not how;
   I can go no longer.'
   'Mark my footsteps, good my page;
   Tread thou in them boldly:
   Thou shalt find the winter's rage
   Freeze thy blood less coldly.'

5. In his master's steps he trod,
   Where the snow lay dinted;
   Heat was in the very sod
   Which the saint had printed.
   Therefore, Christian men, be sure,
   Wealth or rank possessing,
   You who now will bless the poor,
   Shall yourselves find blessing.

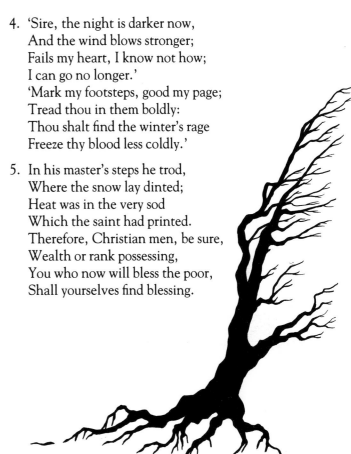

While Shepherds Watched

1. While shepherds watch'd their flocks by night, All seat–ed on the ground, The an–gel of the Lord came down And glor–y shone a–round.

10

2. 'Fear not,' said he: for mighty dread
   Had seized their troubled mind;
   'Glad tidings of great joy I bring
   To you and all mankind.

3. 'To you in David's town this day
   Is born of David's line
   A Saviour, who is Christ the Lord;
   And this shall be the sign:

4. 'The heavenly Babe you there shall find
   To human view displayed,
   All meanly wrapped in swathing bands,
   And in a manger laid.'

5. Thus spake the seraph; and forthwith
   Appeared a shining throng
   Of angels praising God, who thus
   Addressed their joyful song:

6. 'All glory be to God on high,
   And to the earth be peace;
   Good will henceforth from heaven to men
   Begin and never cease.'

The First Nowell

1. The＿ first＿ No – well the＿ Ang – el did say, Was to

cer – tain poor shep – herds in fields as they lay; In＿

fields＿ where＿ they lay＿ keep – ing their sheep, On a

cold win – ter's night＿ that was＿ so deep:

CHORUS

No — well,____ No — well, No — well, No — well,

Born is the King____ of Is — ra — el.

2. They lookèd up and saw a star,
   Shining in the east, beyond them far,
   And to the earth it gave great light,
   And so it continued both day and night:
   Chorus

3. And by the light of that same star,
   Three wise men came from country far;
   To seek for a King was their intent,
   And to follow the star wherever it went:
   Chorus

4. This star drew nigh to the north-west,
   O'er Bethlehem it took its rest,
   And there it did both stop and stay,
   Right over the place where Jesus lay:
   Chorus

5. Then entered in those Wise Men three,
   Full reverently upon their knee,
   And offered there in his presence,
   Their gold and myrrh, and frankincense.
   Chorus

6. Then let us all with one accord,
   Sing praises to our Heavenly Lord,
   That hath made heaven and earth of nought,
   And with his blood mankind hath bought:
   Chorus

Silent Night

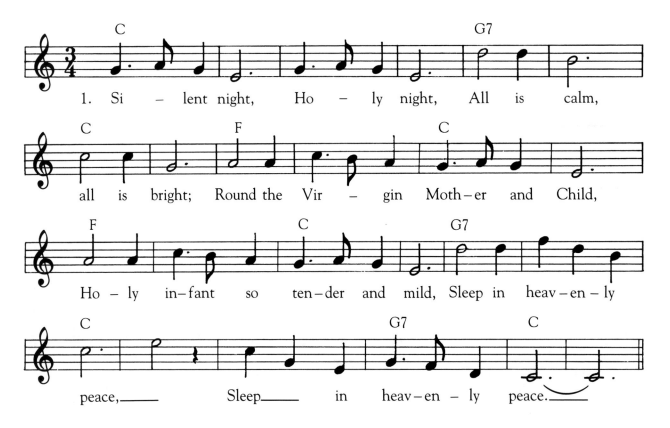

2. Silent night, Holy night,
   Shepherds quake at the sight;
   Glories stream from heaven afar,
   Heavenly hosts sing Alleluya:
   Christ the Saviour is born,
   Christ the Saviour is born.

3. Silent night, Holy night,
   Son of God, love's pure light;
   Radiance beams from thy holy face,
   With the dawn of redeeming grace;
   Jesus, Lord, at thy birth,
   Jesus, Lord, at thy birth.

Away in a Manger

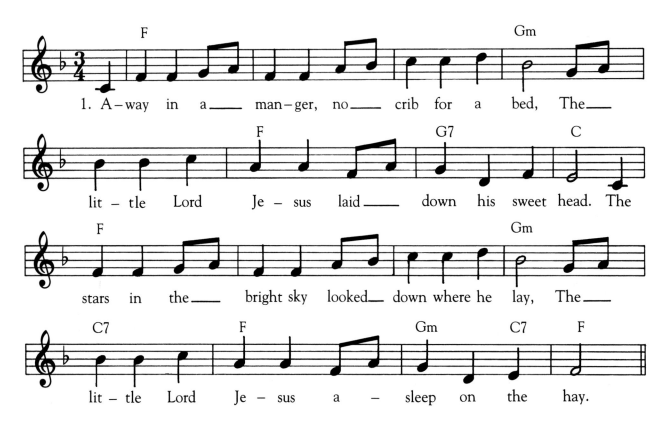

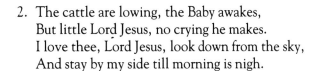

2. The cattle are lowing, the Baby awakes,
   But little Lord Jesus, no crying he makes.
   I love thee, Lord Jesus, look down from the sky,
   And stay by my side till morning is nigh.

3. Be near me, Lord Jesus; I ask thee to stay
   Close by me for ever, and love me, I pray.
   Bless all the dear children in thy tender care,
   And fit us for heaven to live with thee there.

Once in Royal David's City

2. He came down to earth from heaven
   Who is God and Lord of all,
   And his shelter was a stable,
   And his cradle was a stall;
   With the poor and mean and lowly
   Lived on earth our Saviour holy.

3. And through all his wondrous childhood
   He would honour and obey,
   Love and watch the lowly maiden,
   In whose gentle arms he lay;
   Christian children all must be
   Mild, obedient, good as he.

4. For he is our childhood's pattern,
   Day by day like us he grew,
   He was little, weak, and helpless,
   Tears and smiles like us he knew;
   And he feeleth for our sadness,
   And he shareth in our gladness.

5. And our eyes at last shall see him,
   Through his own redeeming love,
   For that child so dear and gentle
   Is our Lord in heaven above;
   And he leads his children on
   To the place where he is gone.

6. Not in that poor lowly stable,
   With the oxen standing by,
   We shall see him, but in heaven,
   Set at God's right hand on high;
   When like stars his children crowned
   All in white shall wait around.

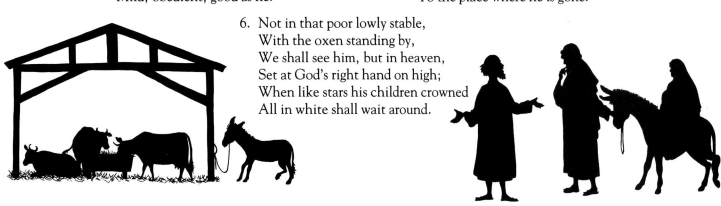

Ding Dong Merrily on High

2. E'en so here below, below
   Let steeple bells be swungen.
   And io, io, io
   By priest and people sungen:
       Chorus

3. Pray you, dutifully prime
   Your matin chime, ye ringers;
   May you beautifully rime
   Your evetime song, ye singers:
       Chorus

Deck the Hall

1. Deck the hall with boughs of hol-ly, Fa la la la   la, la la la la,

'Tis the sea-son   to   be jol-ly, Fa la la la   la, la   la   la   la.

Don we now our   gay ap-par-el,   Fa la   la,   la la la,   la   la   la,

Sing the an-cient Yule-tide ca-rol, Fa la la la   la,   la   la la la.

2. See the blazing Yule before us,
   Fa la la la la, la la la la,
   Strike the harp and join the chorus,
   Fa la la la la, la la la la.
   Follow me in merry measure,
   Fa la la, la la la, la la la,
   While I tell of Yule-tide treasure,
   Fa la la la la, la la la la.

3. Fast away the old year passes,
   Fa la la la la, la la la la,
   Hail the new, you lads and lasses,
   Fa la la la la, la la la la.
   Sing we joyous all together,
   Fa la la, la la la, la la la,
   Heedless of the wind and weather,
   Fa la la la la, la la la la.

Jingle Bells

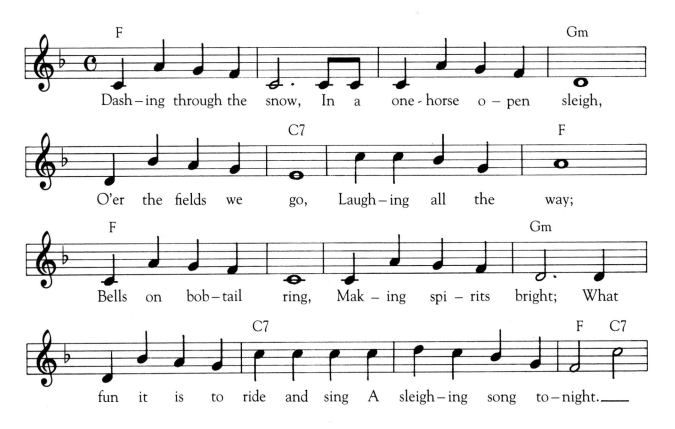

Jin – gle bells, jin – gle bells, Jin – gle all the way,

Oh, what fun it is to ride In a one-horse o – pen sleigh. ____

Jin – gle bells, jin – gle bells, Jin – gle all the way,

Oh, what fun it is to ride In a one-horse o – pen sleigh.

Hark! the Herald Angels Sing

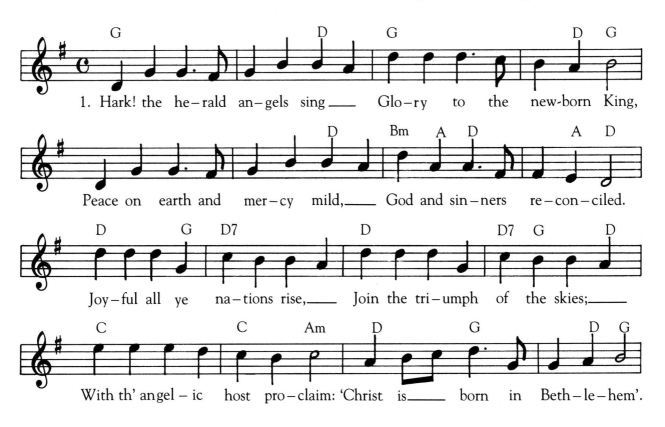

Hark! the he-rald an-gels sing Glo-ry ——— to the new-born King.

2. Christ, by highest Heav'n adored,
Christ, the Everlasting Lord,
Late in time behold him come,
Offspring of a virgin's womb.
Veiled in flesh the Godhead see,
Hail the incarnate Deity!
Pleased as Man with man to dwell,
Jesus, our Emmanuel.
Hark! the herald angels sing
Glory to the new-born King.

3. Hail, the heaven-born Prince of Peace!
Hail, the Sun of Righteousness!
Light and life to all he brings,
Risen with healing in his wings.
Mild he lays his glory by,
Born that man no more may die,
Born to raise the sons of earth,
Born to give them second birth.
Hark! the herald angels sing
Glory to the new-born King.

We Three Kings

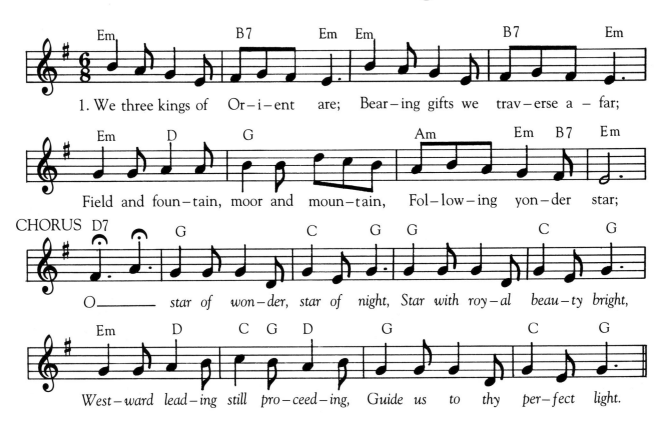

2. *Melchior:*
   Born a king on Bethlehem plain,
   Gold I bring, to crown him again –
   King for ever, ceasing never,
   Over us all to reign:
       Chorus

3. *Caspar:*
   Frankincense to offer have I;
   Incense owns a Deity nigh:
   Prayer and praising, all men raising,
   Worship him, God most high:
       Chorus

4. *Balthazar:*
   Myrrh is mine; its bitter perfume
   Breathes a life of gathering gloom,
   Sorrowing, sighing, bleeding, dying,
   Sealed in the stone-cold tomb:
       Chorus

5. Glorious now, behold him arise;
   King, and God, and sacrifice.
   Heaven sings alleluya,
   Alleluya the earth replies:
       Chorus

Little Donkey

1. Lit – tle don – key, lit – tle don – key, On the dus – ty road.

Got to keep on plod – ding on – wards, With your pre – cious load.

Been a long time, lit – tle don – key, Through the win – ter's night.

Don't give up now, lit – tle don – key, Beth – le – hem's in sight.

CHORUS

Am | Em | D | G | D | G

Ring out those bells to-night, Beth – le – hem, Beth – le – hem.

Am | Em | D | G | D | G

Fol – low that star to-night, Beth – le – hem, Beth – le – hem.

C | F | C | G

Lit – tle don – key, lit – tle don – key, Had a hea – vy day.

C | F | G | C

Lit – tle don – key, car – ry Ma – ry safe – ly on her way.

2. Little donkey, little donkey,
   On the dusty road.
   There are wise men, waiting for a
   Sign to bring them here.

Do not falter, little donkey,
There's a star ahead.
It will guide you, little donkey,
To a cattle shed.   *Chorus*

The Little Drummer Boy

1. 'Come', they told me, Pa- rum- pa- pum- pum,_____

'Our new-born King to see! Pa- rum- pa- pum- pum,_____

Our fin—est gifts we bring, Pa- rum- pa- pum- pum,_____

To lay be – fore the King! Pa- rum- pa- pum- pum,

Rum- pa- pum- pum, rum- pa- pum- pum,_____

So to honour Him, Pa- rum-pa-pum- pum,___ When_ we come.___

2. 'Little Baby, Pa-rum-pa-pum-pum,
I am a poor boy too, Pa-rum-pa-pum-pum,
I have no gift to bring, Pa-rum-pa-pum-pum,
That's fit to give our King! Pa-rum-pa-pum-pum,
Rum-pa-pum-pum, rum-pa-pum-pum,
Shall I play for You, Pa-rum-pa-pum-pum,
On my drum?'

3. Mary nodded, Pa-rum-pa-pum-pum,
The ox and lamb kept time, Pa-rum-pa-pum-pum,
I played my drum for Him, Pa-rum-pa-pum-pum,
I played my best for Him, Pa-rum-pa-pum-pum,
Rum-pa-pum-pum, rum-pa-pum-pum,
Then He smiled at me, Pa-rum-pa-pum-pum,
Me and my drum!

See, Amid the Winter's Snow

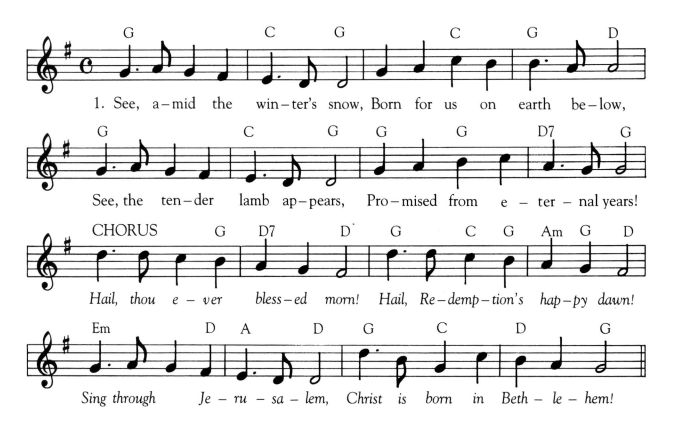

1. See, a–mid the win–ter's snow, Born for us on earth be–low,
See, the ten–der lamb ap–pears, Pro–mised from e – ter – nal years!

CHORUS
Hail, thou e – ver bless—ed morn! Hail, Re–demp–tion's hap–py dawn!
Sing through Je – ru – sa – lem, Christ is born in Beth – le – hem!

2. Lo, within a manger lies
   He who built the starry skies,
   He who, throned in height sublime,
   Sits amid the cherubim!
   Chorus

3. Say, ye holy shepherds, say,
   What your joyful news today;
   Wherefore have ye left your sheep
   On the lonely mountain steep?
   Chorus

4. 'As we watched at dead of night,
   Lo, we saw a wondrous light;
   Angels singing "Peace on earth"
   Told us of the Saviour's birth.'
   Chorus

5. Sacred infant, all divine,
   What a tender love was Thine,
   Thus to come from highest bliss
   Down to such a world as this!
   Chorus

6. Teach, O teach us, holy child,
   By Thy face so meek and mild,
   Teach us to resemble Thee
   In Thy sweet humility.
   Chorus

The Three Drovers

2. The black swans flew across the sky,
   The wild dog called across the plain,
   The starry lustre blazed on high,
   Still echoed on the Heavenly strain;
   And still they sang, 'Noel; Noel!'
   Those drovers three, 'Noel! Noel!
   Noel! Noel! Noel!'

3. The air was dry with Summer heat
   And smoke was on the yellow Moon;
   But from the Heavens, faint and sweet,
   Came floating down a wond'rous tune
   And as they heard, they sang full well,
   Those drovers three, 'Noel! Noel!
   Noel! Noel! Noel!'

The Holly and the Ivy

1. The hol-ly and the i-vy, When they are both full grown, Of__
all the trees that are in the wood, The__ hol-ly bears the crown.

CHORUS
O The ris-ing of the sun __ And the run-ning of the deer, The__
play-ing of the merr-y or-gan, Sweet sing-ing in the choir.

2. The holly bears a blossom,
   As white as the lily flower,
   And Mary bore sweet Jesus Christ
   To be our sweet Saviour:
   Chorus

3. The holly bears a berry,
   As red as any blood,
   And Mary bore sweet Jesus Christ
   To do poor sinners good:
   Chorus

4. The holly bears a prickle,
   As sharp as any thorn,
   And Mary bore Sweet Jesus Christ
   On Christmas day in the morn:
   Chorus

5. The holly bears a bark,
   As bitter as any gall,
   And Mary bore sweet Jesus Christ
   For to redeem us all:
   Chorus

6. The holly and the ivy,
   When they are both full grown,
   Of all the trees that are in the wood,
   The holly bears the crown:
   Chorus

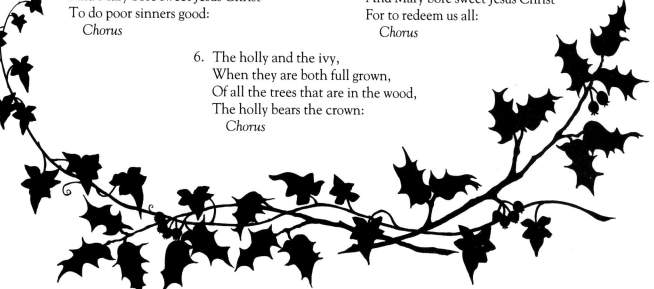

I Saw Three Ships

2. And what was in those ships all three?
   On Christmas Day, etc.

3. Our Saviour Christ and his lady.
   On Christmas Day, etc.

4. Pray, whither sailed those ships all three?
   On Christmas Day, etc.

5. O, they sailed into Bethlehem.
   On Christmas Day, etc.

6. And all the bells on earth shall ring.
   On Christmas Day, etc.

7. And all the angels in Heaven shall sing.
   On Christmas Day, etc.

8. And all the souls on earth shall sing.
   On Christmas Day, etc.

9. Then let us all rejoice amain!
   On Christmas Day, etc.

O Come, All Ye Faithful

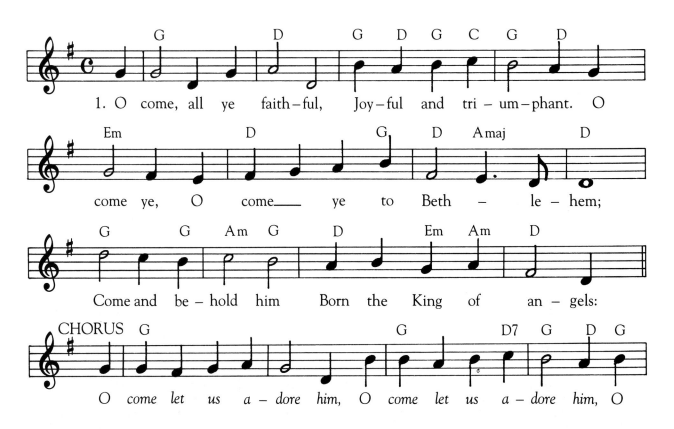

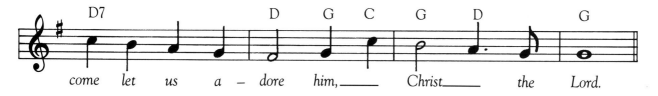

come let us a – dore him,____ Christ____ the Lord.

2. God of God,
   Light of Light,
   Lo, he abhors not the Virgin's womb;
   Very God,
   Begotten not created:
      Chorus

3. Sing choirs of angels,
   Sing in exultation,
   Sing, all ye citizens of heaven above;
   Glory to God
   In the highest:
      Chorus

4. Yea, Lord, we greet thee,
   Born this happy morning.
   Jesu, to thee be glory given;
   Word of the Father,
   Now in flesh appearing:
      Chorus

God Rest You Merry Gentlemen

1. God rest you mer-ry gen-tle-men, Let no-thing you dis-
-may. Re-mem-ber Christ our Sa - viour Was born on Christmas
day, To save our souls from Sa-tan's power When we were gone a-
-stray: O_____ tid-ings of com - fort and joy, Comfort and

joy, O— ti – dings of com — fort and joy.

2. In Bethlehem in Jewry
This blessed Babe was born,
And laid within a manger
Upon this blessed morn,
The which his Mother Mary
Did nothing take in scorn:
Chorus

3. From God our heavenly Father
A blessed angel came,
And unto certain shepherds
Brought tidings of the same,
How that in Bethlehem was born
The son of God by name:
Chorus

4. 'Fear not' then said the angel,
'Let nothing you affright;
This day is born a Saviour
Unto a Virgin bright
To free all you who trust in him
From Satan's power and might':
Chorus

5. The shepherds at these tidings
Rejoicèd much in mind,
And left their flocks a-feeding
In tempest, storm, and wind,
And went to Bethlehem straightway
The Son of God to find:
Chorus

6. Now when they came to Bethlehem
Whereat the Infant lay,
They found him in a manger
Where oxen feed on hay;
His Mother Mary kneeling down
Unto the Lord did pray:
Chorus

7. Now to the Lord sing praises
All you within this place,
And with true love and brotherhood
Each other now embrace;
This holy tide of Christmas
All others doth deface:
Chorus

O Little Town of Bethlehem

2. For Christ is born of Mary;
   And, gathered all above,
   While mortals sleep, the angels keep
   Their watch of wondering love.
   O, morning stars, together
   Proclaim the holy birth,
   And praises sing to God the King
   And peace to men on earth.

3. How silently, how silently,
   The wondrous gift is given!
   So God imparts to human hearts
   The blessings of his heaven.
   No ear may hear his coming;
   But in this world of sin,
   Where meek souls will receive him, still
   The dear Christ enters in.

4. O holy Child of Bethlehem,
   Descend to us, we pray;
   Cast out our sins, and enter in:
   Be born in us today.
   We hear the Christmas angels
   The great glad tidings tell:
   O come to us, abide with us,
   Our Lord Emmanuel.

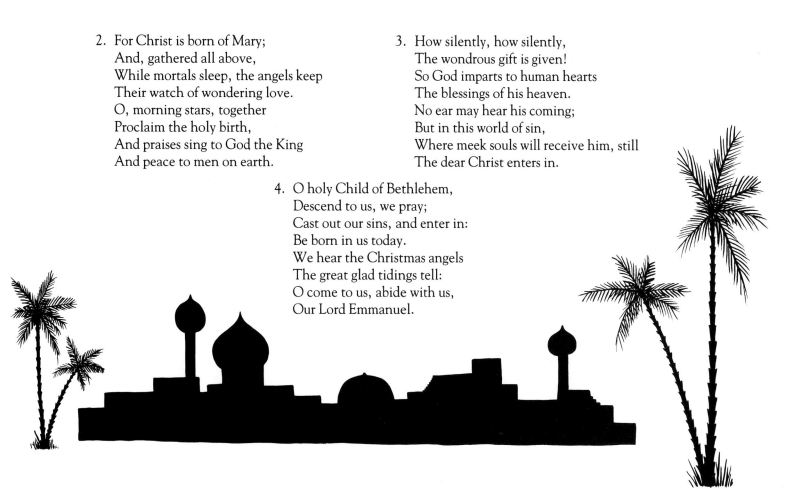

Acknowledgements

The publishers are grateful to the following for granting permission to include copyrighted material in this collection:

Page 30: 'Little Donkey' © Chappell Music Ltd, London W1Y 3SA
Reproduced by permission of Chappell Music Ltd & International Music Publications.

Page 32: 'The Little Drummer Boy' © 1958 Mills Music Inc & International Korwin Corp, USA.
Chappell Music Ltd, London W1Y 3SA
Reproduced by permission of Chappell Music Ltd & International Music Publications.

Page 36: 'The Three Drovers' © 1948 by Chappell & Co (Australia) Pty Ltd trading as Warner/Chappell Music.
International copyright Secured. All Rights Reserved.

Page 46: 'Forest Green' (melody line of 'O Little Town of Bethlehem') from the *English Hymnal* by permission of Oxford University Press.

Compiled by Elizabeth Small & Lucy Duke.

Every effort has been made to trace and acknowledge copyright owners. If any right has been omitted, the author and publishers offer their apologies and will rectify this in subsequent editions following notification.